t

Say these **t** words out loud. Then write

truck

tent

What sound does **t** make? Make the sound.
Now sound out these words.

tin   **tap**   **ten**

i

These words have the **i** sound in the middle.
Say the words out loud. Then write the **i**'s.

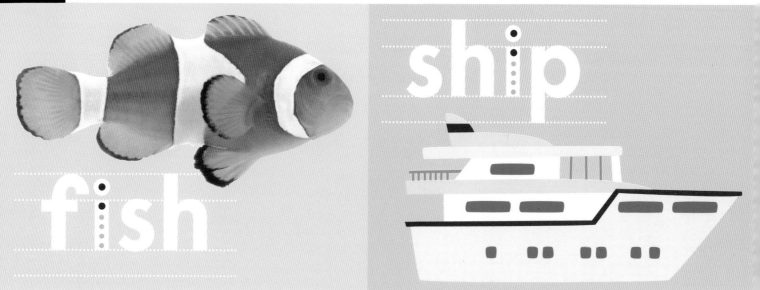

fish

ship

What sound does **i** make? Make the sound.
Now sound out these words.

bit   **kiss**   **rip**

Say these **p** words out loud. Then write the **p**'s.

pie

pencil

What sound does **p** make? Make the sound.
Now sound out these words.

pit   **pad**   **pet**

o These words have the **o** sound in the middle.
Say the words out loud. Then write the **o**'s.

fox

frog

What sound does **o** make? Make the sound.
Now sound out these words.

hop   **top**   **cot**

n Say these **n** words out loud. Then write the **n**'s.

nest

nose

What sound does **n** make? Make the sound.
Now sound out these words.

nap **nut** **nod**

e These words have the **e** sound in the middle.
Say the words out loud. Then write the **e**'s.

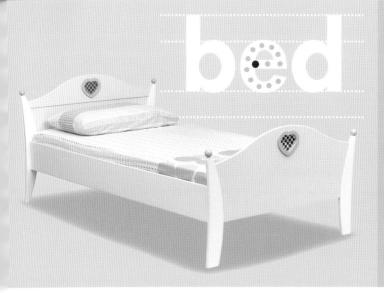

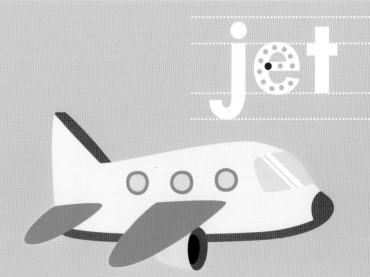

bed

jet

What sound does **e** make? Make the sound.
Now sound out these words.

wet **ten** **red**

m

Say these **m** words out loud. Then write the **m**'s.

mouse

mug

What sound does **m** make? Make the sound.
Now sound out these words.

miss **man** **met**

u

These words have the **u** sound in the middle.
Say the words out loud. Then write the **u**'s.

rug

puppy

What sound does **u** make? Make the sound.
Now sound out these words.

run **hut** **nut**

d Say these **d** words out loud. Then write the **d**'s.

dog   duck

What sound does **d** make? Make the sound.
Now sound out these words.

dot   **dip**   **dad**

g Say these **g** words out loud. Then write the **g**'s.

goat   guitar

What sound does **g** make? Make the sound.
Now sound out these words.

gill   gas   get

c

Say these **c** words out loud. Then write the **c**'s.

cat

car

What sound does **c** make? Make the sound.
Now sound out these words.

can   **cot**   **cap**

k

Say these **k** words out loud. Then write the **k**'s.

kick

king

What sound does **k** make? Make the sound.
Now sound out these words.

keep   **kit**   **kid**

Say these **r** words out loud. Then write the **r**'s.

rabbit **radio**

What sound does **r** make? Make the sound.
Now sound out these words.

rap   **red**   **rot**

h Say these **h** words out loud. Then write the **h**'s.

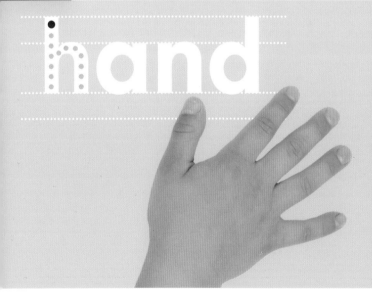 

hand **horse**

What sound does **h** make? Make the sound.
Now sound out these words.

her   **hot**   **him**

b

Say these b words out loud. Then write the b's.

ball

boot

What sound does **b** make? Make the sound.
Now sound out these words.

bat   **bun**   **bit**

f

Say these f words out loud. Then write the f's.

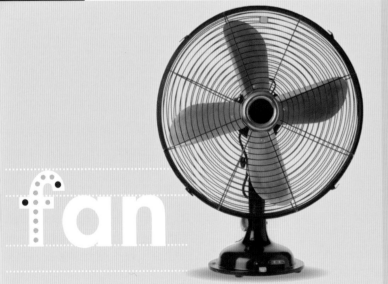

fan

fish

What sound does **f** make? Make the sound.
Now sound out these words.

fat   **fed**   **fig**

lion

lamp

What sound does **l** make? Make the sound.
Now sound out these words.

lap   **led**   **lip**

j Say these **j** words out loud. Then write the **j**'s.

jump

jeep

What sound does **j** make? Make the sound.
Now sound out these words.

jig   jet   job

10

V Say these **v** words out loud. Then write the **v**'s.

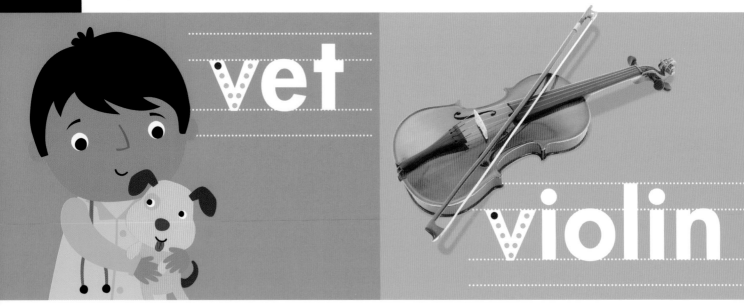

vet

violin

What sound does **v** make? Make the sound.
Now sound out these words.

van

vat

vest

W Say these **w** words out loud. Then write the **w**'s.

wig

wagon

What sound does **w** make? Make the sound.
Now sound out these words.

win

wall

well

Say these words with **x** in them out loud.
Then write the **x**'s.

box   six

What sound does **x** make? Make the sound.
Now sound out these words.

wax   **fix**   **mix**

y Say these **y** words out loud. Then write the **y**'s.

yak   yacht

What sound does **y** make? Make the sound.
Now sound out these words.

yes   **yap**   **yet**   12

z

Say these **z** words out loud. Then write the **z**'s.

zoo

ZOO

zigzag

What sound does **z** make? Make the sound.
Now sound out these words.

zip   **zap**   **zoom**

q

Say these **q** words out loud. Then write the **q**'s.

quilt

quiet

What sound does **q** make? Make the sound.
Now sound out these words.

quit   **quad**   **quiz**

Can you remember the sounds?
Write the first letter in each word.

[ ]ion

[ ]ock

[ ]all

[ ]orse

[ ]uppy

[ ]ruck

14

Ready Set Learn

First Phonics

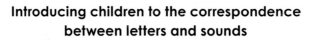

The early years are an important period in children's learning and a vital stepping stone for their success in school. This wipe-clean workbook provides teacher-approved activities to help children in important curriculum areas. The wipe-clean pages mean children can practise again and again, and build confidence while they learn.

Dealing with letters in the order recommended by phonics experts, this book focuses on:

Introducing children to the correspondence between letters and sounds

•

Tracing lower-case letters

•

Developing dexterity

Encourages reading skills

Help children to say each word aloud as they write. This develops their reading and spelling skills.

Promotes writing skills

Give children plenty of practice in forming letters. Wipe the pages clean and allow children to repeat them until they are confident.

Promotes hand-eye coordination

Tracing and writing activities help develop children's hand-eye coordination.

Illustrated by Charly Lane

CE

£5.99

Copyright © 2020
make believe ideas ltd
The Wilderness, Berkhamsted, Hertfordshire, HP4 2AZ, UK.

Recommended for children aged 3 years and over.
Manufactured in China.
www.makebelieveideas.co.uk

ISBN10: 1-78947-641-0
ISBN13: 978-1-78947-641-5

9 781789 476415

02202001